POEMS FOR ME
THAT SPELLS MAGIC

POEMS FOR ME
THAT SPELLS MAGIC

chosen by
TONY BRADMAN

Illustrated by Madeleine Baker

BLACKIE

British Library Cataloguing in Publication Data

That spells magic
1. Children's poetry in English.
Special subjects: Magic – Anthologies
I. Bradman, Tony II. Series
821'. 008'037

ISBN 0-216-92739-0

Blackie and Son Ltd
7 Leicester Place
London WC2H 7BP

Typeset by
Jamesway Graphics
Hanson Close
Middleton
Manchester M24 2HD

Printed in Great Britain

This is a book of magic spells,
Of wizards and witches and cauldrons as
  well,
Of things that are scary, that bump in
  the night,
That howl in the darkness and give you a
  fright.
There are witches on broomsticks, ghosts
  galore,
Two who are tiny, one at the door;
There's a house that is haunted, a dog on
  a shelf,
And a teacher who isn't quite feeling
  herself.
Creepy things happen, things move
  around . . .
What's that in the garden? And what is
  that sound?
A goblin is sitting out there by the gate
And somewhere a troll is lying in wait . . .
But don't be too frightened, it isn't all
  scary,
If you're careful and quiet you might
  meet a fairy.
There's magic around you, wherever you
  look . . .
But especially here, inside this book!

Tony Bradman

The Ghost of Number Twenty-four

The ghost of number twenty-four
Doesn't half knock on the door.
He knocks all day,
He knocks all night,
He doesn't half give me a fright.

I wonder if everyone knows
We've a ghost living here.
I'd better tell them to steer clear.
But they all started asking,
'Is it big, fat or thin?'
But I'll tell you something —

He doesn't half knock on the door!

Hussein Thompson
(Age 11)

I Like To Stay Up

I like to stay up
and listen
when big people talking
jumbie stories

I does feel
so tingly and excited
inside me

But when my mother say
'Girl, time for bed'

Then is when
I does feel a dread

Then is when
I does jump into me bed

Then is when
I does cover up
from me feet to me head

Then is when
I does wish I didn't listen
to no stupid jumbie story

Then is when
I does wish I did read
me book instead

('Jumbie' is a Guyanese word for 'ghost')

Grace Nichols

Teeny Tiny Ghost

A teeny tiny ghost
no bigger than a mouse
at most,
lived in a great big house.

It's hard to haunt
a great big house
when you're a teeny tiny ghost
no bigger than a mouse,
at most.

He did what he could do.

So every dark and stormy night —
the kind that shakes a house with
    fright —
if you stood still and listened right,
you'd hear a
teeny
tiny
BOO!

Lilian Moore

Three Ghostesses

Three little ghostesses,
Sitting on postesses,
Eating buttered toastesses,
Greasing their fistesses,
Up to their wristesses,
Oh, what beastesses
To make such feastesses!

Anon

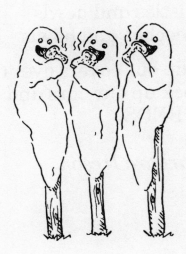

The Small Ghostie

When it's late and it's dark
And everyone sleeps . . . shhh shhh shhh.

Into our kitchen
A small ghostie creeps . . . shhh shhh
  shhh,

We hear knockings and raps
And then rattles and taps,

Then he clatters and clangs
And he batters and bangs,

And he whistles and yowls
And he screeches and howls . . .

So we pull up our covers over our heads
And we block up our ears and WE STAY
  IN OUR BEDS.

Barbara Ireson

House Ghosts

Airing cupboard ghosts
hold music practices
inside the water tank.

Television ghosts
poke crooked fingers
across your favourite programmes.

Chimney ghosts
sing one note songs
over and over in owly voices.

Vacuum cleaner ghosts
roar and the dust obeys them,
into the bag.

But the worst ghost
hides under your bed at night!
When everything's quiet
you can hear him breathing.

Irene Rawnsley

Haunted House

There's a house upon the hilltop
We will not go inside
For that is where the witches live,
Where ghosts and goblins hide.

Tonight they have their party,
All the lights are burning bright,
But oh we will not go inside
The haunted house tonight.

The demons there are whirling
And the spirits swirl about.
They sing their songs to Hallowe'en.
'Come join the fun,' they shout.

But we do not want to go there
So we run with all our might
And oh we will not go inside
The haunted house tonight.

Jack Prelutsky

Hallowe'en

Bring a candle!
  Bring a light —
It must be Hallowe'en
  Tonight!

I saw a pixie
  small and fine
dancing
  on the washing line . . .

I saw a witch
  go riding high
on her broomstick
  through the sky . . .

I saw a giant
  ten feet wide
With half a dozen
  ships inside . . .

I saw a fairy
  like a dream
top the milk
  and sip the cream . . .

I saw a goblin
    plump and brown
turn the church clock
    upside down!

Come as quickly
    as you can —
I saw the back
    of a bogy man!

Jean Kenward

The Hour When the Witches Fly

When the night is as cold as stone,
When lightning severs the sky,
When your blood is chilled to the bone,
That's the hour when the witches fly.

When the night-owl swoops for the kill,
When there's death in the fox's eye,
When the snake is coiled and still,
That's the hour when the witches fly.

When the nightmares scream in your
     head,
When you hear a strangled cry,
When you startle awake in your bed,
That's the hour when the witches fly.

When the sweat collects on your brow,
When the minutes tick slowly by,
When you wish it was then not now,
That's the hour when the witches fly.

John Foster

Shrieks At Midnight

I do like ogres —
There's something about them
So utterly ruthless
And yet absurd!
    I don't believe in them.
Yet I shiver
The very instant
I hear the word —
FE-FI-FO-FUM!

Dorothy Brown Thompson

19

Halloween

'Granny, I saw a witch go by
I saw two, I saw three!
I heard their skirts go swish, swish,
   swish —'

   'Child, 'twas leaves against the sky,
   And the autumn wind in the tree.'

'Granny, broomsticks they bestrode,
Their hats were black as tar,
And buckles twinkled on their shoes —'

   'You saw but shadows on the road,
   The sparkle of a star.'

'Granny, all their heels were red,
Their cats were big as sheep.
I heard a bat say to an owl —'

   'Child, you must go straight to bed,
   'Tis time you were asleep.'

'Granny, I saw men in green,
Their eyes shone fiery red,
Their heads were yellow pumpkins —'

'Now you've told me what you've seen,
'WILL you go to bed?'

'Granny?'

'Well?'

'Don't you believe — ?'

'What?'

'What I've seen?
Don't you know it's Halloween?'

Marie A Lawson

The Witch's Brew

Hubble bubble at the double
Cooking pot stir up some trouble.

Into my pot
there now must go
leg of lamb
and green frog's toe,

and men's socks
and dirty jeans,
a rotten egg
and cold baked beans.

Hubble bubble at the double
Cooking pot stir up some trouble.

One dead fly
and a wild wasp's sting,
the eye of a sheep
and the heart of a King;

a stolen jewel
and mouldy salt,
and for good flavour
a jar of malt.

Hubble bubble at the double
Cooking pot stir up some trouble.

Wing of bird
and head of mouse,
screams and howls
from that haunted house.

And don't forget
the jug of blood
or the sardine tin
or the clod of mud.

Hubble bubble at the double
Cooking pot stir up
SOME
TROUBLE!

Wes Magee

On Halloween

We mask our faces
and wear strange hats
and moan like witches
and screech like cats
and jump like goblins
and thump like elves
and almost manage
to scare *ourselves*.

Aileen Fisher

Hallowe'en Indignation Meeting

A sulky witch and a surly cat
And a scowly owl and a skeleton sat
With a grouchy ghost and a waspish bat,
And angrily snarled and chewed the fat.

It seems they were all upset and riled
That they couldn't frighten the Modern
   Child,
Who was much too knowing and much
   too wild
And considered Hallowe'en spooks
   too mild.

Said the witch, 'They call this the *human*
   race,
Yet the kiddies inhabit Outer Space;
They bob for comets, and eat ice-cream
From flying saucers, to get up steam!'

'I'm a shade of my former self,' said the
   skeleton.
'I shiver and shake like so much gelatin,
Indeed I'm a pitiful sight to see—
I'm scareder of *kids* than they are of *me*!

Margaret Fishback

The Wizard Said:

'You find a sheltered spot that faces
    south . . .'
'And then?'
'You sniff and put two fingers in your
    mouth . . .'
'And then?'
'You close your eyes and roll your
    eye-balls round . . .'
'And then?'
'You lift your left foot slowly off the
    ground . . .'
'And then?'
'You make your palm into a kind of
    cup . . .'

'And then?'
'You *very quickly* raise your right foot
up . . .'
'And then?'
'You fall over.'

Richard Edwards

Superstitions

Wash your hands in the moonlight,
don't step on any crack;
cross your fingers,
cross your toes,
touch wood to keep your luck.

Always watch for black cats,
wear odd socks unawares;
choose sevens or threes,
'Bless you!' when you sneeze,
and never cross on stairs.

Remember these with all you've got;
if not . . .

Judith Nicholls

Spellbound

Wednesday we went to a Magic Show
   For Timothy's birthday treat.
This bloke pulled a rabbit out of his hat
   And two pigeons from under his feet.

There were card tricks and rope tricks
   and magic screens
   That made somebody disappear.
But the best was the man in the seat
   next to me,
   Who had hair growing out of his ear!
It was MAGIC!!

Hazel Townson

The Conjurer

He magicked a spider,
He magicked a bat,
He magicked two doves,
That flew out of his hat.

I said, 'But that's small stuff!'
He tried once again,
But all that he magicked
Was a bantam hen.

I looked down my nose.
'Do you call that *big*?' —
He puffed and he strained
And he magicked a pig.

'That's more like it!' I said,
'But I've seen an old witch,
Magic whales as big
As a football pitch!

'*You* couldn't magic a
Small tiger,' I bet him.
But he *did*. — And to prove it
The tiger ATE HIM!

Raymond Wilson

Wizard

Under my bed I keep a box
With seven locks,

And all the things I have to hide
Are safe inside:

My rings, my wand, my hat, my shells,
My book of spells.

I could fit a mountain into a shoe
If I wanted to,

Or put the sea in a paper cup
And drink it up.

I could change a cushion into a bird
With a magic word,

Or turn December into Spring,
Or make stones sing.

I could clap my hands and watch the
    moon,
Like a white balloon,

Come floating to my window-sill . . .

One day I will.

Richard Edwards

And for my next trick

Out of his hat he pulled a hen
that laid a shining egg, and when
he broke the egg with his white-tipped
   wand
it became an eye in the palm of his
hand.

And when the eye had looked around
he swallowed it without a sound.

At which the hen, with a polite
bow, put on the hat, and went off,
   stage right.

And everyone clapped; though my
   sister said
she wished it had been a duck;
for the magican stood there in the
   spotlight
all feathers and beaky head
going
cluck
cluck
cluck

Dave Calder

School Visit

The Great Merlanda's here today
with tricks and traps and spells;
there's not a murmur in the hall,
you'd hear a speck of stardust fall
except

    for Jim

       who
fidgets, fiddles,
whispers, wriggles,
sniggers, giggles,
won't sit still

      till

       at last

The Great Merlanda,
footsteps ringing,
cloak a-swinging,
strides right down
past seated pupils
reaches Jim's row,
simply yells . . .

**IF YOU DON'T SIT IN YOUR CHAIR,
  BOY,**

I'll . . .

turn you into a rabbit
and stuff you in my hat,
I'll lock you up in my bottomless box
or places worse than that!
I'll turn you into the six of spades
and deal you out to the Head;
I'll saw you in two then tie up the bits
in a granny-knot, I said!
I'll turn you into a handkerchief
or a mouse to play with my cat!
If you can't sit still
    RIGHT NOW
        on that chair . . .
Said Jim,
   'I'll do just that!'

Judith Nicholls

As If By Magic

I don't like the way
things move about
secretly, when
you're not looking.

You can leave a pen
on your school desk,
turn to your friend
for a second, it's gone;

pencil sharpeners,
rubbers are the same,
always taking
magic holidays.

In the cloakroom
when no one's there
I think the coats and shoes
have a party,

play hide-and-seek,
dance with each other.
They rush back to the racks
when the bell sounds

but you can tell
what's been going on.
Nothing is ever in the place
where you left it.

Irene Rawnsley

The Number

There is a magic number
And if you say it standing on your head,
Your dreams will all come true,
Your old things will be new,
You'll never cry
Or sit alone and sigh.

I found it out by chance
While upside down against the garden
   shed.
I can't give it away,
I'm not allowed to say,
But here's a clue:
It isn't sixty-two.

Richard Edwards

I Feel Creepy

I feel creepy tonight
I wonder what's wrong

the night feels like a snake
that just turned itself
inside out

I feel creepy
I keep looking over my shoulder

turnstare! turnstare!
turnsssssssssssssssssss
ssssssssssssssssstare!

Martin Hall

That Spells Magic

Ever since we started
Our project on witches
Teacher's behaviour
Has been getting

Strange

This morning, for example,
She flew in through
The window on a broomstick
Looped the loop
Over our heads
Cackled a lot, produced
From her cloak
A cat, four bats and two rats
(One alive, one dead)
And a lizard's gizzards
Then she drew in the air
Letters of fire two feet high,
An A, and a G, and an M,
And a C and an I . . .
They all did a dance
While we sat entranced
And arranged themselves
Into a word

That spells magic said she
and disappeared
In a cloud of smoke.

Now isn't that
The strangest thing
You've ever heard?

Tony Bradman

Fairy Grandmother

My grandmother
wore cobweb clothes
and knitted spells
from thistledown.
Princesses
came to her for beauty,
frogs to be changed;
her fairy duty
flew her to far-off palaces
in distant countries.

I'm small for my age.
Mum gives me pills;
wishes I'd grow
like other girls.
The dentist
put a brace on my teeth
so I don't talk much.
I watch the stars breathe
when I'm in bed
and hear in my head
Grandmother's stories.

Irene Rawnsley

Dancing in the Street

Last night I couldn't get to sleep.
Some ghosts were dancing in the street.
I saw them through my window pane.
The way they twirled and whirled,
Then twirled back again,
Made them look just like Mum's sheets
Gusting in the wind and the rain. . .

Michael Glover

I'd love To Be a Fairy's Child

Children born of fairy stock
Never need for shirt or frock,
Never want for food or fire,
Always get their heart's desire:
Jingle pockets full of gold,
Marry when they're seven years old,
Every fairy child may keep
Two strong ponies and ten sheep;
All have houses, each his own,
Built of brick or granite stone;
They live on cherries, they run wild —
I'd love to be a fairy's child.

Robert Graves

The China Dog

He lives by himself in a shelf in our hall,
But he never barks when people call;
He never teases for cake at tea,
Or wags his tail at sight of me,
Stiffly it curls about his back,
Where the spots are painted brown and
    black.
He has a sad, unblinking eye
And I always pat him when I go by.

If I knew the magic words to say
He would leave that shelf this very day!
He'd not be a china dog at all,
Solemn and stiff against a wall,
But he'd bark and follow me everywhere
And nip my fingers and lick my hair,
While every single night he'd be
Snuggled up warm in bed with me!

Rachel Field

The Rainbow Fairies

Two little clouds one summer's day,
   Went flying through the sky;
They went so fast they bumped their
   heads,
   And both began to cry.

Old Father Sun looked out and said:
   'Oh, never mind, my dears,
I'll send my little fairy folk
   To dry your falling tears.'

One fairy came in violet,
   And one wore indigo;
In blue, green, yellow, orange, red,
   They made a pretty row.

They wiped the cloud-tears all away,
  And then from out the sky,
Upon a line the sunbeams made,
  They hung their gowns to dry.

Anon

If You See a Fairy Ring

If you see a fairy ring
  In a field of grass,
Very lightly step around,
  Tiptoe as you pass;
Last night fairies frolicked there,
And they're sleeping somewhere near.

If you see a tiny fay
  Lying fast asleep,
Shut your eyes and run away,
  Do not stay to peep;
And be sure you never tell,
Or you'll break a fairy spell.

Anon

Bad Tooth Fairy

My tooth came out on Friday.
   On Saturday I found
That underneath my pillow
   It had turned into a pound!
'Tooth fairy!' all the class cried.
   I gave a pitying smirk.
'You can't believe in stuff like that!
   It simply doesn't work.
It's just my dad; he's loaded!
   I'll tell you what I'll do —
You give me all the teeth you lose
   And I'll go halves with you.'
James brought me one on Tuesday.
   (Great! Fifty pence apiece!)
Two more turned up by Thursday night
   From Darren and Denise.

But then on Friday morning
I had a nasty fright —
One set of vampire dentures,
And not a coin in sight!

Hazel Townson

Fairies

Don't go looking for fairies,
They'll fly away if you do.
You never can see the fairies
Till they come looking for you.

Eleanor Farjeon

Sea Fairies

They're hiding by the pebbles,
   They're running round the rocks.
Each of them and all of them
   In dazzling sea-green frocks.

They're gathering strips of sea-weed,
   The ribands fair that lie
Along the winding water-mark
   The tide has left so high.

They're flying with the sand,
   They're singing in the caves,
And dancing in the white foam
   They toss from off the waves.

But if you try to catch them
   They're always out of reach —
Not everywhere and anywhere,
   But somewhere on the beach.

Eileen Mathias

Found In The Woods

I found a little brown purse
   The fairies left for me,
It was stitch'd with green and yellow,
   As pretty as could be.
It was full of fairy money,
   As full as it could be,
So I bought a pot of honey
   And had it for my tea.

Irene F Pawsey

Merry Little Men

Down in the grassy hollow
   Live merry little men.
On moonlight nights they frolic — but
   They don't come out till ten.

And I'm in bed by seven,
   And so I don't know when
I'll go and play with them —
   They don't come out till ten!

Kathleen M Chaplin

The Elf

I know an elf
And an elf knows me . . .
He lives in our garden
Behind the tree.

You don't believe me?
It's true, I swear.
I *know* an elf
Is living there.

I know because
Just last week
I climbed that tree
And heard a creak.

I heard a whistle,
I heard a hiss,
I saw a glow —
And made a wish.

I wished and wished
With all my might
And kept my fingers
Crossed all night.

I wished for something
I'd really like . . .
And for my birthday
I got a bike.

I know an elf
And an elf knows me.
He heard me wishing
Up that tree.

Perhaps he'll hear
Your wishes, too . . .
It's worth a try,
I think — don't you?

Tony Bradman

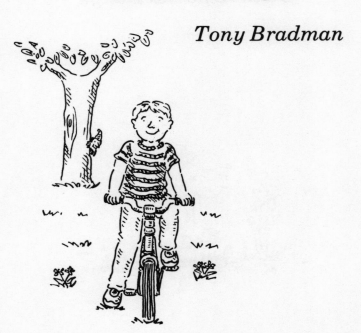

The Little Elf

I met a little Elf man, once,
    Down where the lilies blow.
I asked him why he was so small,
    And why he didn't grow.

He slightly frowned, and with his eye
    He looked me through and through.
'I'm quite as big for me,' said he,
    'As you are big for you.'

John Kendrick Bangs

The Goblin

There's a goblin as green
As a goblin can be
Who is sitting outside
And is waiting for me.

When he knocked on my door
And said softly, 'Come play.'
I answered, 'No thank you,
Now, please, go away.'

But the goblin as green
As a goblin can be
Is still sitting outside
And is waiting for me.

Jack Prelutsky

The Goblin

A goblin lives in our house, in our house,
    in our house,
A goblin lives in our house all the year
    round.

        He bumps
        And he jumps
        And he thumps
        And he stumps.
        He knocks
        And he rocks
        And he rattles at the
            locks.

A goblin lives in our house, in our house,
    in our house,
A goblin lives in our house all the year
    round.

Rose Fyleman

The Troll

Be wary of the loathsome troll
that slyly lies in wait
to drag you to his dingy hole
and put you on his plate.

His blood is black and boiling hot,
he gurgles ghastly groans.
He'll cook you in his dinner pot,
your skin, your flesh, your bones.

He'll catch your arms and clutch your
   legs
and grind you to a pulp,
then swallow you like scrambled eggs —
gobble! gobble! gulp!

So watch your steps when next you go
Upon a pleasant stroll,
Or you might end in the pit below
as supper for the troll.

Jack Prelutsky

from The Fairies

Up the airy mountain,
　　Down the rushy glen,
We daren't go a-hunting,
　　For fear of little men;
Wee folk, good folk,
　　Trooping all together;
Green jacket, red cap,
　　And white owl's feather!

They stole little Bridget
　　For seven years long;
When she came down again
　　Her friends were all gone.
They took her lightly back,
　　Between the night and morrow,
They thought that she was fast asleep
　　But she was dead with sorrow.
They have kept her ever since
　　Deep within the lakes,
On a bed of flag-leaves,
　　Watching till she wakes.

Up the airy mountain,
  Down the rushy glen,
We daren't go a-hunting
  For fear of little men;
Wee folk, good folk,
  Trooping all together;
Green jacket, red cap,
  And white owl's feather!

William Allingham

My Dragon

I have a purple dragon
With a long brass tail that clangs,
And anyone not nice to me
Soon feels his fiery fangs,

So if you tell me I'm a dope
Or call my muscles jelly,
You just might dwell a billion years
Inside his boiling belly.

X J Kennedy

60

Vanishing Trick

I've just found out I may have a magic
    tongue.
(Worrying, in one so young!)
And if you think that's a tall tale to tell,
I'm probably afflicted with magic teeth,
    as well!
Oh, you can sneer! But actually it's
    quite tragic,
Not knowing for sure which bit of me is
    magic.
It could be my throat, my neck, or even
    my whole head.
All I know for sure, is 'That cake
disappeared by magic!' my
mum said.

Hazel Townson

Index of First Lines

Acknowledgements

The Publishers and author would like to thank the following for their kind permission to reproduce copyright material in this book:

Dave Calder for 'And For My Next Trick' © Dave Calder 1988 by permission of the Author; William Collins Ltd for 'Merry Little Men' by Kathleen M Chaplin; Lutterworth Press for 'The Wizard Said', 'Wizard' and 'The Number' by Richard Edwards; David Higham Associates for 'Fairies' by Eleanor Farjeon; Doubleday for 'The China Dog' by Rachel Field from *Taxis* and *Toadstools* © 1926, 1924 Yale Publishing Co, 1926 Crowell Publishing Co; Random House for 'Halloween Indignation Meeting' by Margaret Fishback from *Poems Made Up To Take Out* © 1963; Heinemann for 'On Halloween' by Aileen Fisher; John Foster for 'The Hour When the Witches Fly'; Michael Glover for 'Dancing in the Street' © 1988; Evans Brothers Ltd for 'I'd love to Be a Fairy's Child' by Robert Graves; Martin Hall for 'I Feel Creepy'; Century Hutchinson for 'The Small Ghostie' by Barbara Ireson; Curtis Brown Ltd for 'My Dragon' by X J Kennedy © 1975, 1977, 1978, 1979 by X J Kennedy; Jean Kenward for 'Hallowe'en'; Child Life Magazine copyright 1936, 1962 by Rand McNally and Co for 'Halloween' by Marie A Lawson; Wes Magee for 'The Witch's Brew' © Wes Magee, as author; Scholastic for 'Teeny, Tiny Ghost' by Lilian Moore from *Spooky Rhymes and Riddles*; Curtis Brown Ltd on behalf of Grace Nichols copyright © 1988 Grace Nichols for 'I Like to Stay Up'; Judith Nicholls for 'School Visit' © 1989. Reprinted by permission of the author; Faber and Faber for 'Superstitions' by Judith Nicholls from *Midnight Forest;* Greenwillow Books for 'The Goblin' by Jack Prelutsky; A & C Black and William Morrow & Co for 'The Troll' by Jack Prelutsky from *Nightmares*; World's Work and Greenwillow Books for 'Haunted House' by Jack Prelutsky; Irene Rawnsley for 'As If By Magic', 'House Ghosts' and 'Fairy Grandmother'; Bell & Hyman for 'Shrieks at Midnight' by Dorothy Brown Thompson; Hussein Thompson for 'The Ghost of Number Twenty-Four', Hazel Townson for 'Spellbound', 'Bad Tooth Fairy' and 'Vanishing Trick'; Raymond Wilson for 'The Conjurer'.

Every effort has been made to trace copyright holders and the Publishers and author apologize if any inadvertent omission has been made.